The KidHaven Health Library

What Happens When Someone Has
DEPRESSION?

By Katie Kawa

KidHaven
PUBLISHING

Published in 2020 by
KidHaven Publishing, an Imprint of Greenhaven Publishing, LLC
353 3rd Avenue
Suite 255
New York, NY 10010

Designer: Andrea Davison-Bartolotta
Editor: Katie Kawa

Photo credits: Cover (main) Andrey_Popov/Shutterstock.com; cover, back cover, interior (background texture) Oksancia/Shutterstock.com; pp. 5, 20 Monkey Business Images/ Shutterstock.com; p. 7 (bottom) Africa Studio/Shutterstock.com; pp. 7 (top), 25 fizkes/ Shutterstock.com; pp. 8–9 Sergey Mironov/Shutterstock.com; p. 9 (top left) Sabphoto/ Shutterstock.com; p. 9 (top right) Have a nice day Photo/Shutterstock.com; pp. 9 (bottom right), 21, 22 wavebreakmedia/Shutterstock.com; p. 10 Kiwis/Shutterstock.com; p. 12 joshya/ Shutterstock.com; p. 13 Blamb/Shutterstock.com; p. 14 Viktoriia Hnatiuk/Shutterstock.com; p. 15 Rawpixel.com/Shutterstock.com; p. 16 (bottom left, bottom right) Tinseltown/Shutterstock.com; p. 16 (top) JStone/Shutterstock.com; p. 17 Antonio Guillem/Shutterstock.com; p. 18 Alex Studio/ Shutterstock.com; p. 19 Image Point Fr/Shutterstock.com; p. 23 New Africa/Shutterstock.com; p. 24 Nikodash/Shutterstock.com; p. 26 Prostock-studio/Shutterstock.com; p. 29 Pressmaster/ Shutterstock.com.

Library of Congress Cataloging-in-Publication Data

Names: Kawa, Katie, author.
Title: What happens when someone has depression? / Katie Kawa.
Description: First edition. | New York : KidHaven Publishing, [2020] | Series: The KidHaven health library | Includes bibliographical references and index.
Identifiers: LCCN 2019015984 (print) | LCCN 2019019574 (ebook) | ISBN 9781534532557 (eBook) | ISBN 9781534532434 (library bound book) | ISBN 9781534532571 (pbk. book) | ISBN 9781534532649 (6 pack)
Subjects: LCSH: Depression, Mental–Juvenile literature. | Depression, Mental–Etiology–Juvenile literature. | Mental health–Juvenile literature.
Classification: LCC RC537 (ebook) | LCC RC537 .K3987 2020 (print) | DDC 616.85/27–dc23
LC record available at https://lccn.loc.gov/2019015984

Printed in the United States of America

Some of the images in this book illustrate individuals who are models. The depictions do not imply actual situations or events.

CPSIA compliance information: Batch #BW20KL: For further information contact Greenhaven Publishing LLC, New York, New York at 1-844-317-7404.

Please visit our website, www.greenhavenpublishing.com. For a free color catalog of all our high-quality books, call toll free 1-844-317-7404 or fax 1-844-317-7405.

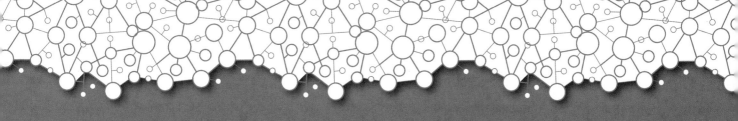

Contents

MORE THAN SADNESS

Everyone feels sad sometimes. For most people, sadness goes away after a while. They can talk to a friend, do a favorite activity, or even get some sleep and feel better.

For some people, though, sadness doesn't go away that easily. They don't have any interest in doing things that used to make them happy. When people feel like this for a long time, they aren't just in a bad mood. They have a health problem called depression.

Many people deal with depression at some point in their lives, so it's important to know what it is and how people with it can get the help they need. With the right **treatment** and support from family and friends, people with depression can get better.

Different Names for Depression

What we commonly call depression also goes by other names. Doctors often call it major depressive disorder. A disorder is another name for a health problem. This disorder is also sometimes called clinical depression. These names show that depression is a serious medical problem that requires treatment from a doctor or another medical **professional**.

Feeling sad isn't the same thing as having depression. Doctors can tell if a person has depression by looking for certain signs and how long they've lasted. Doctors can also help people find the right treatment so they can feel better.

MENTAL HEALTH MATTERS!

Depression is one of many mental illnesses, or mental disorders, that affect millions of people around the world. Mental illnesses affect how a person thinks, feels, and acts because they affect the brain.

In the past, some people believed that mental illnesses weren't as serious as physical illnesses, which affect the body. However, as people have learned more about mental health, they've come to understand that people with mental illnesses such as depression need support and medical treatment just like people with the flu or another physical illness.

Some people feel uncomfortable talking about having depression or other mental illnesses, but there's nothing to be

Fighting the Stigma

People sometimes feel ashamed of having depression because there's still a stigma around mental illnesses. A stigma is a **negative** view surrounding something that's often unfair and not based in facts. However, many people are working to fight back against the stigma surrounding depression and other mental illnesses. By talking respectfully about mental health and treating all people with kindness, everyone can do their part to help those with mental illnesses feel supported.

ashamed of. With any health problem—mental or physical—talking openly about it can help educate people and can encourage others to get help.

A mental illness such as depression is a real and serious illness, just like the flu. This means it often needs to be treated in the same way a physical illness is treated—with visits to doctors and medicines to help the person feel better.

SIGNS OF DEPRESSION

Depression affects how people think and feel in different ways. Sadness that doesn't go away is one major sign of depression, but many people with depression often have trouble feeling anything. They often say they feel empty. Things that used to make them feel good, such as playing sports or reading, don't interest them anymore.

Sometimes people with depression feel hopeless and think or say unkind things about themselves. Depression can also make some people angry. Young people with depression are especially quick to get mad, frustrated, or **annoyed**.

Depression affects the brain in other ways too. It can make it hard for people to think and focus on things at school or work. Making decisions can also be hard for people with depression.

Problems with Sleep

People with depression often have problems sleeping. In some cases, they sleep too much. Other people with depression deal with insomnia, which means they can't sleep or get very little sleep for reasons they can't control. Sometimes, people with depression wake up too early and can't get back to sleep. None of these problems on their own mean someone has depression, but if someone is having problems with sleep for a long time, it's good to talk to a doctor about it.

Many people with depression believe things will never get better for them, but that's not true. Depression tricks their brain into believing the worst instead of seeing that there are many reasons to hope.

Even though depression is a mental illness, it can still cause physical problems. A common sign of depression is feeling tired all the time without knowing why. People with depression often feel like they don't have enough energy to do basic tasks, such as taking a shower or changing their clothes. Some days, it can be hard for them to find the energy to go to work or school or even to get out of bed.

Depression can also affect how people eat. People with depression sometimes don't feel hungry or don't have the energy to make or get food, so they lose weight. Other people with depression eat too much and aren't very active, so they gain weight.

Depression Can Hurt

In some cases, depression can cause pain in different parts of a person's body. For example, it can cause someone's head or stomach to hurt. Depression can cause other stomach problems too. It can take doctors a long time to figure out these problems are caused by depression because they often have to rule out other causes and try other treatments first.

SIGNS OF DEPRESSION

feeling sad, hopeless, empty, or angry

feeling worthless

having no energy

These are some of the most common signs of depression. A person generally needs to show many of these signs nearly all the time for at least two weeks before a doctor can **diagnose** them with major depressive disorder.

physical problems and pains that don't have any other cause and don't go away with other treatment

having no interest in things that were once enjoyed

having trouble focusing and making decisions

changes in weight and in how much a person eats

sleep problems

DEPRESSION AND THE BRAIN

What causes depression? There isn't one easy answer, but studying the brain is a good place to start. Scientists believe chemicals in the brain, called neurotransmitters, play a part in many mental disorders, including depression. These chemicals help messages travel from one neuron, or nerve cell, to another. The messages allow the brain and body to work together to do many things—from walking and talking to dealing with different emotions.

Synapse

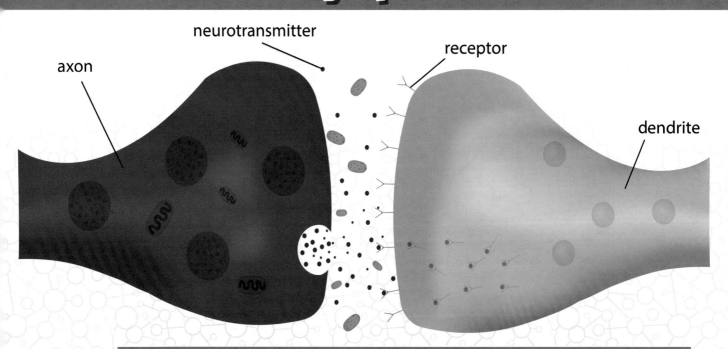

axon

neurotransmitter

receptor

dendrite

Neurotransmitters help messages travel across the space between neurons, which is called a synapse. The message moves down the long part of the nerve called the axon, travels across the synapse, and is received by the end, or dendrite, of the next neuron. This process doesn't always work correctly in a person with depression.

People with depression often have low levels of certain neurotransmitters that help balance their moods. This includes serotonin, which helps a person feel good. Scientists believe some people with depression don't produce enough of these neurotransmitters or aren't able to receive messages from them correctly.

A Changing Brain

Depression can affect the size of parts of the brain. For example, studies have shown that the part of the brain that deals with memories—the hippocampus—is smaller in some people with depression. Scientists believe this may be caused by the **stress** of being depressed, which can keep new cells from growing. On the other hand, the part of the brain that deals with strong emotions—the amygdala—is sometimes larger in people with depression.

amygdala

hippocampus

A COMBINATION OF CAUSES

Many things can affect a person's chance of **developing** depression. Low levels of brain chemicals play a part in depression, but other things play a part too. Scientists are studying how certain genes are connected to depression. Genes are the parts of cells that control different **traits**, such as eye color. Genes are passed down from parents to children. Because depression often runs in families, scientists believe certain genes might make a person more likely to develop depression.

Family History

Many health problems, including depression, run in families. This means if a parent or grandparent has a health problem, their children or grandchildren are more likely to have it too. This is why it's important for people to talk openly about their family medical history. When you know your family history, you can do a better job of watching for signs of health problems that might run in your family.

Depression can also be triggered, or brought on, by a sad life event, such as the death of a family member or moving away from a support system. In addition, physical health problems, especially ones that last for a long time, can sometimes cause a person to become depressed.

Scientists believe depression isn't caused by just one thing. For example, family problems can lead to depression in people whose genes make them more likely to develop this disorder.

WHO'S AFFECTED?

Depression is one of the most common mental health problems in the world. It affects more than 300 million people worldwide. In the United States, more than 17 million adults had one or more major depressive episodes, or periods of major depressive disorder, in 2017. Women are almost twice as likely as men to be diagnosed with depression, but it affects people of all genders, as well as people of all races and backgrounds.

Famous Names

Some of the most famous people in the world have struggled with depression, and they've shared their stories to help fight the stigma surrounding this disorder. Lady Gaga, Selena Gomez, Beyoncé, and Dwayne Johnson are just some of the people who've opened up about dealing with depression. In addition, Kristen Bell, who's an actress and the voice of Princess Anna in the *Frozen* movies, has talked openly about taking medicine to help with her depression.

Lady Gaga

Selena Gomez

Dwayne Johnson

Depression is an illness that can develop no matter how much money a person makes or how successful they appear. It's not helpful to tell someone with depression that they shouldn't be depressed because they have a good life.

People of all ages can develop depression too. Although it's most often diagnosed in adults, children and teens can develop depression. In fact, around 3 percent of young people between the ages of 3 and 17 have been diagnosed with depression in the United States.

DIFFERENT KINDS OF DEPRESSION

Major depressive disorder isn't the only kind of depression. Some people deal with signs of depression, such as a lack of interest in activities and feelings of sadness, for months or even years. When someone shows these signs for at least two years, they can be diagnosed with persistent depressive disorder. This is also known as dysthymia.

Another kind of depression is seasonal affective disorder, which is sometimes shortened to SAD. People with SAD often

Helping New Moms

Postpartum depression affects new moms. It involves feelings of sadness and worry that are so strong a woman can't properly care for herself or her baby. However, there are many treatments that can help women with this kind of depression feel better. Women are starting to talk about this problem more openly than ever before. This is leading many new moms to get the help they need.

show signs of depression only in the fall and winter, when there's less sunlight. These signs often go away in spring and summer. If someone has SAD, they can sit near a special light during times of the year with less sunlight. This often helps them feel better.

It's important for people who think they might have dysthymia, SAD, or another kind of depression to talk to their doctor. A doctor can help them find treatments that work best for them, such as the use of a light **therapy** box for SAD.

GETTING HELP

No matter what kind of depression a person is living with, there's help available for them. However, it can sometimes be hard for someone with depression to ask for help. They might not have the energy to talk to someone about what they're going through. They might also be afraid that someone will judge them or think less of them because of how they feel. It's important for them to know that getting help for their depression is a sign of strength and not weakness.

A doctor often asks about a person's mood, energy levels, physical health, and family history before diagnosing them with depression.

Talking to a trusted family member or friend is often the first step. The next step is seeing a doctor. Depression is an illness, and only a doctor can officially diagnose someone with depression and help them get the right treatment.

Different Doctors

Some people with depression get help from their regular doctor or see another kind of mental health professional who's not a doctor. However, many people with depression see a kind of doctor called a psychologist, who can help them in many ways but can't give them medicine. If they need medicine to treat their depression, they can only get that from a medical doctor, such as a psychiatrist.

TALK
ABOUT IT

Talking about your problems can often help you feel better. This is why many doctors suggest that people with depression try a kind of treatment called talk therapy. This kind of therapy is led by a psychologist, psychiatrist, or other mental health professional, who's often called a therapist. It's their job to help a person with depression find healthy ways to deal with negative thoughts and problems in their lives.

Other Treatments

Exercise has been shown to help people with depression feel better. It gives people a rush of positive feelings and can help people sleep better too. In addition, people with depression sometimes find that meditation helps them. This relaxing practice involves focusing on what's happening in the moment and learning to notice negative thoughts without letting them control you. Meditation has been shown to change the brain in ways that help it better handle stress.

A person with depression often meets with their therapist in a one-on-one setting. However, family therapy can be helpful for some people, especially when children are affected by depression.

Because people tell their therapist private things about their lives, trust and comfort are important. It can take a few tries for a person to find the right therapist for them.

Different therapists are trained to work with different kinds of patients. For example, some therapists work only with children and teens.

MEDICINE FOR DEPRESSION

Depression is often treated with a combination of talk therapy and medicine. Drugs used to treat depression are called antidepressants, and many different kinds of antidepressants exist. In general, these drugs work by changing the way the brain makes or uses certain chemicals, such as serotonin. When these chemicals are able to work the way they should, a person with depression often feels better.

Kids and Antidepressants

The brain of a kid is different than the brain of an adult. It's still developing. Because of this, antidepressants can affect kids and teens differently than they affect adults. If a doctor believes a young person needs an antidepressant, they often watch them closely at first to make sure the medicine isn't affecting them in a negative way. However, some antidepressants have been shown to be very helpful for young people with depression.

It can take time for a person with depression to find the right medicine or amount of medicine—also known as dosage—that works for them. Antidepressants often take weeks to work before a person starts feeling better, so it's important to stick with the treatment and to never stop taking an antidepressant unless a doctor says it's okay.

Medicine is an important part of treating many different health problems, including depression.

OFFERING SUPPORT

Depression doesn't just affect the person who has it. It also affects their family and friends. It can be hard to see someone you love deal with depression, but there are many things you can do to help them.

Learning more about depression can help you understand what they're going through. People with depression need support, so sometimes simply listening to them or spending time with them can help them feel better.

What Not to Say

Someone with depression has an illness, so speaking to them as if they can control their thoughts often only makes things worse. For example, people with depression are sometimes told, "You don't have any reason to be sad. Other people have it worse." This makes the person with depression feel guilty. It's also not helpful to suggest thinking positively or to tell them to stop thinking negative thoughts about themselves. That's like telling someone with a cold to stop sneezing.

In some cases, people with depression don't have the energy to do certain tasks. You can ask if they need help washing dishes or doing other things around the house. You can also ask them if they want to take a walk or play a game together.

How can you help someone with depression?

! Learn more about the signs of depression.

! Listen when they talk about what they're going through.

! Spend time with them, and invite them to do things they once enjoyed.

! Remind them that they're loved.

! Treat them with respect.

! Go for a walk or take part in another kind of exercise with them.

These are just some of the ways you can show someone with depression that you care about them. If you think someone you know might have depression, talk to a trusted adult about how to get them the help they need.

REASONS TO HOPE

Depression isn't an easy thing to deal with. However, there are many treatments that can help people with this disorder live healthy and happy lives. It all starts with being brave enough to ask for help.

If you've been feeling sad, angry, or empty for a long time or don't have the energy to do things you used to enjoy, talk to a trusted adult about what you're feeling. It's always good to talk openly about your thoughts and feelings with someone you trust. This can help your mental health in important ways throughout your life.

A healthy brain is just as important as a healthy body, and when we learn more about mental health issues, such as depression, we're better prepared to help others—and ourselves.

A Month for Mental Health

May is Mental Health Month. Starting in 1949, people have used this month to call attention to mental health issues, such as depression, throughout the United States. During this month, many people share their stories of mental health issues and treatment. This educates people and can help end the stigma surrounding mental illness.

28

Depression may make some people feel hopeless, but there are plenty of reasons to hope. Therapy, medicine, and the support of family and friends can make life much better for someone living with depression.

Glossary

annoyed: Slightly angry, often because of a repeated action.

develop: To cause something to change, happen, be built, or be created over time.

diagnose: To identify a disease by its signs and symptoms.

negative: Harmful or bad.

professional: A person who does a job that requires special education or skill.

stress: A state of strong feelings of worry.

therapy: A method used to treat a mental or physical health problem.

trait: A quality that makes one person or thing different from another.

treatment: Care given to a person or animal that is sick.

WEBSITES

KidsHealth: Feelings

kidshealth.org/en/kids/feeling

This part of the KidsHealth website deals with different emotions and issues surrounding mental health, including what happens in talk therapy.

NAMI: StigmaFree

www.nami.org/stigmafree

The National Alliance on Mental Illness (NAMI) has tips for fighting the stigma surrounding mental illnesses such as depression, as well as a quiz to see how the negative views of mental illness have affected you.

BOOKS

Dorwick, Christopher, and Susan Martin. *Can I Tell You About Depression?: A Guide for Friends, Family, and Professionals.* Philadelphia, PA: Jessica Kingsley Publishers, 2015.

Duhig, Holly. *A Book About Depression.* Norfolk, England: BookLife Publishing, 2018.

Poole, Hilary W. *Depression.* Broomall, PA: Mason Crest, 2016.